GRAPHIC LIBRARY

GRAPHIC SCIENCE

EXPLORING ECOSYSTEMS WITH MAX AXIOM SUPER SCIENTIST

by Agnieszka Biskup
illustrated by Tod Smith

Consultant:
Dr. Ronald Browne
Associate Professor of Elementary Education
Minnesota State Univeristy, Mankato

Capstone press
Mankato, Minnesota

Graphic Library is published by Capstone Press,
1710 Roe Crest Drive, North Mankato, Minnesota 56003.
www.capstonepub.com

Printed in the United States of America in North Mankato, Minnesota.
052012
006767R

Books published by Capstone Press are manufactured with paper containing at least 10 percent post-consumer waste.

Library of Congress Cataloging-in-Publication Data
Biskup, Agnieszka.
Exploring ecosystems with Max Axiom, super scientist / by Agnieszka Biskup; illustrated by Tod Smith.
p. cm.—(Graphic library. Graphic science)
Includes bibliographical references and index.
ISBN-13: 978-0-7368-6842-6 (hardcover)
ISBN-10: 0-7368-6842-9 (hardcover)
ISBN-13: 978-0-7368-7894-4 (softcover pbk.)
ISBN-10: 0-7368-7894-7 (softcover pbk.)
1. Ecology—Juvenile literature. I. Smith, Tod, ill. II. Title.
QH541.14B57 2007
577—dc22 2006029490

Summary: In graphic novel format, follows the adventures of Max Axiom as he explains the science behind ecosystems.

Art Director and Designer
Bob Lentz and Thomas Emery

Cover Artist
Tod Smith

Colorist
Matt Webb

Editor
Donald Lemke

Photo illustration credit: Corel, 17

TABLE OF CONTENTS

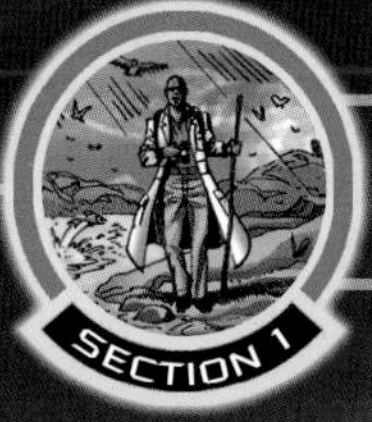
SECTION 1

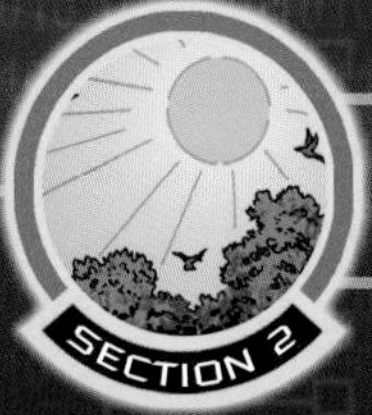
SECTION 2

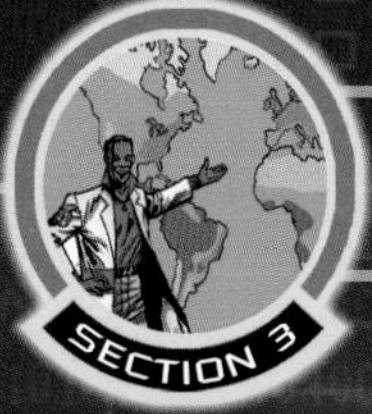
SECTION 3

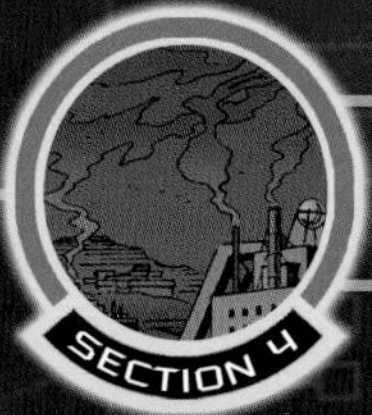
SECTION 4

All organisms, big and small, are connected. Each depends upon other living things to survive.
That's right, Max! Many animals eat plants for energy to live.
Some survive by eating other animals.
And not just when they're dangling from a cliff! Right, Teresa?
The earth is also full of things that aren't alive.
Like sunlight, which gives plants energy to make food.

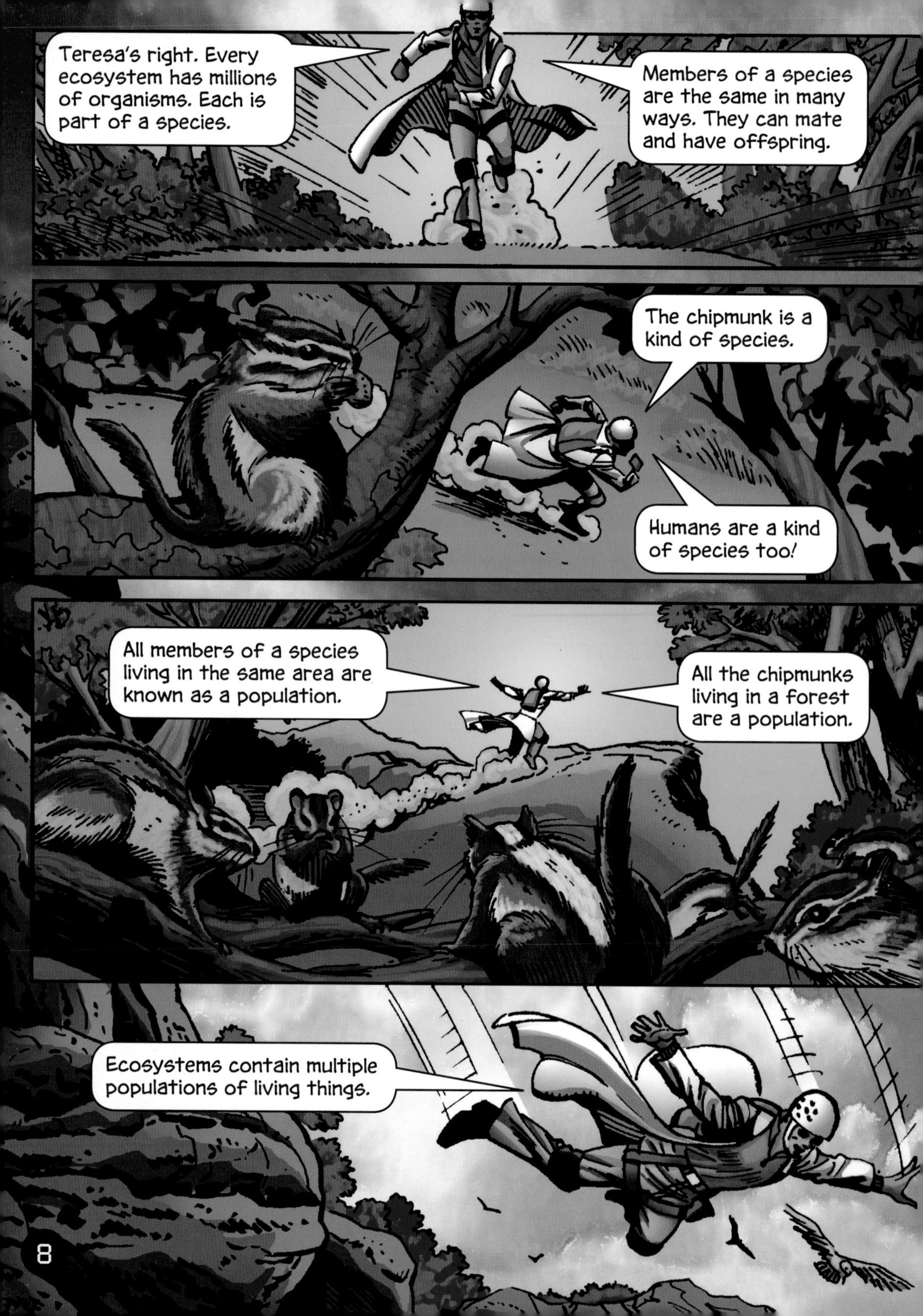
Teresa's right. Every ecosystem has millions of organisms. Each is part of a species.
Members of a species are the same in many ways. They can mate and have offspring.
The chipmunk is a kind of species.
Humans are a kind of species too!
All members of a species living in the same area are known as a population.
All the chipmunks living in a forest are a population.
Ecosystems contain multiple populations of living things.

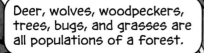

Deer, wolves, woodpeckers, trees, bugs, and grasses are all populations of a forest.

They depend on each other for food and shelter. Together they're known as a community.

The community and its nonliving environment form an ecosystem.

The earth is made up of a variety of ecosystems, all linked and working together.

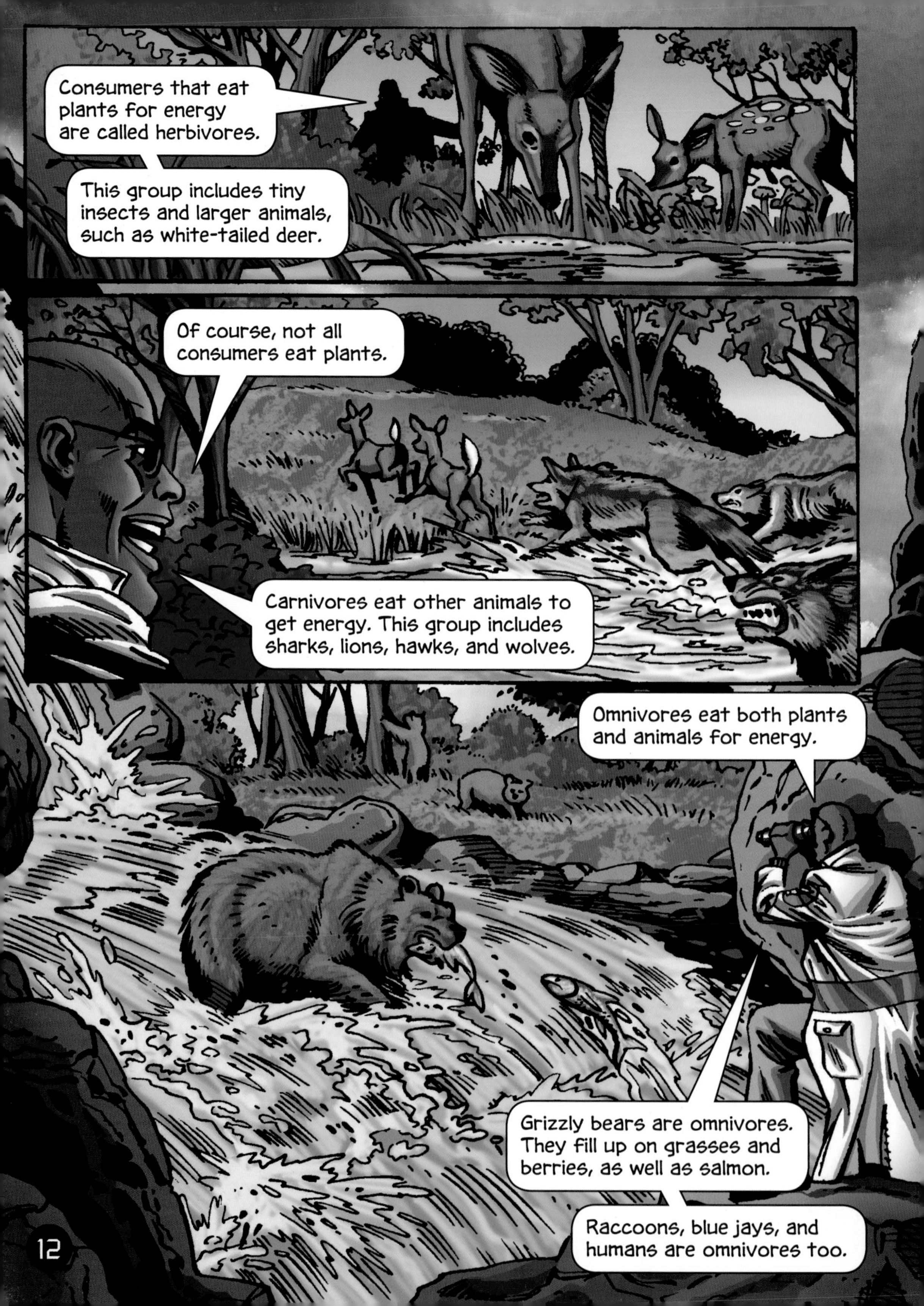
Consumers that eat plants for energy are called herbivores.
This group includes tiny insects and larger animals, such as white-tailed deer.
Of course, not all consumers eat plants.
Carnivores eat other animals to get energy. This group includes sharks, lions, hawks, and wolves.
Omnivores eat both plants and animals for energy.
Grizzly bears are omnivores. They fill up on grasses and berries, as well as salmon.
Raccoons, blue jays, and humans are omnivores too.

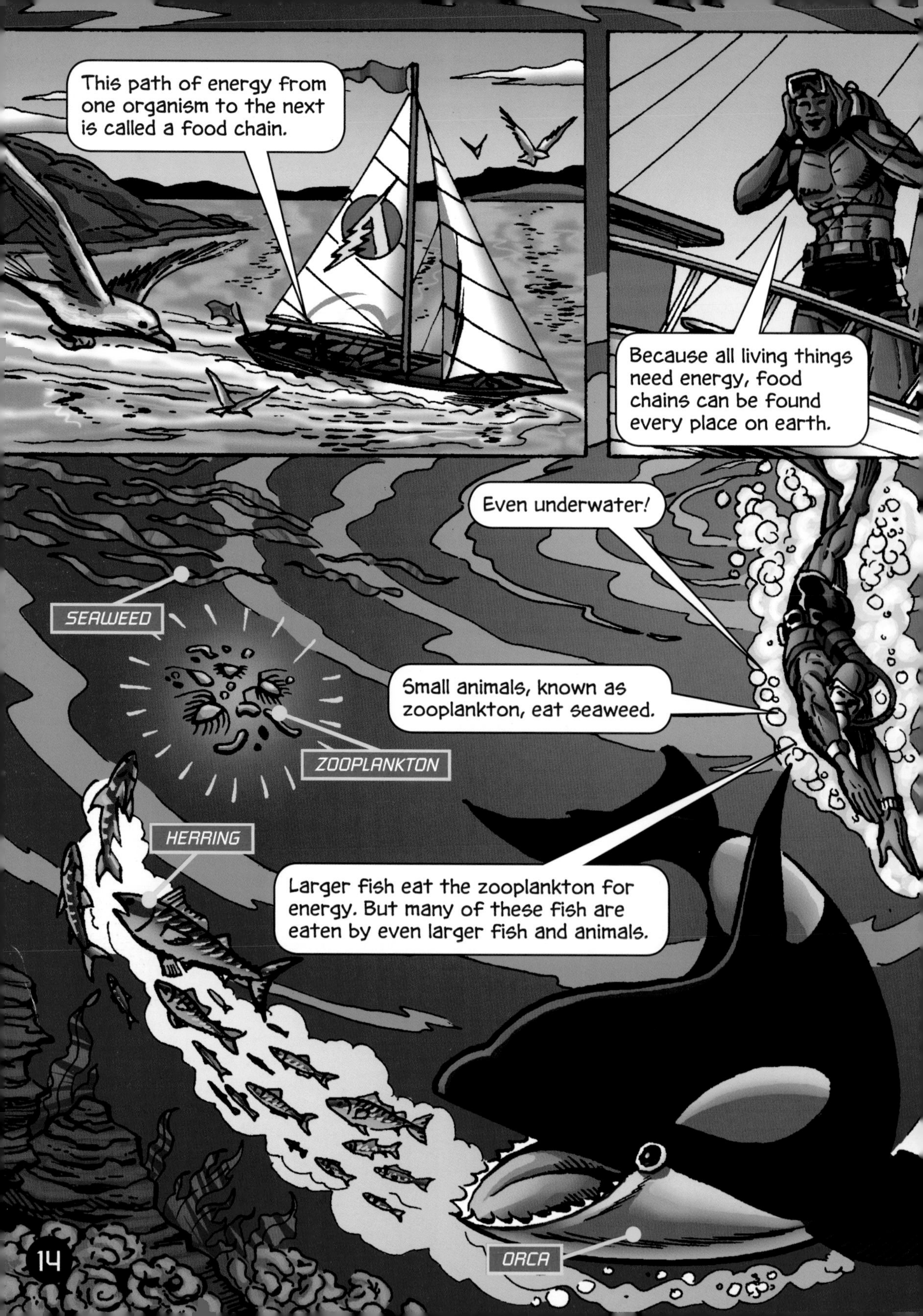
This path of energy from one organism to the next is called a food chain.
Because all living things need energy, food chains can be found every place on earth.
Even underwater!
SEAWEED
Small animals, known as zooplankton, eat seaweed.
ZOOPLANKTON
HERRING
Larger fish eat the zooplankton for energy. But many of these fish are eaten by even larger fish and animals.
ORCA

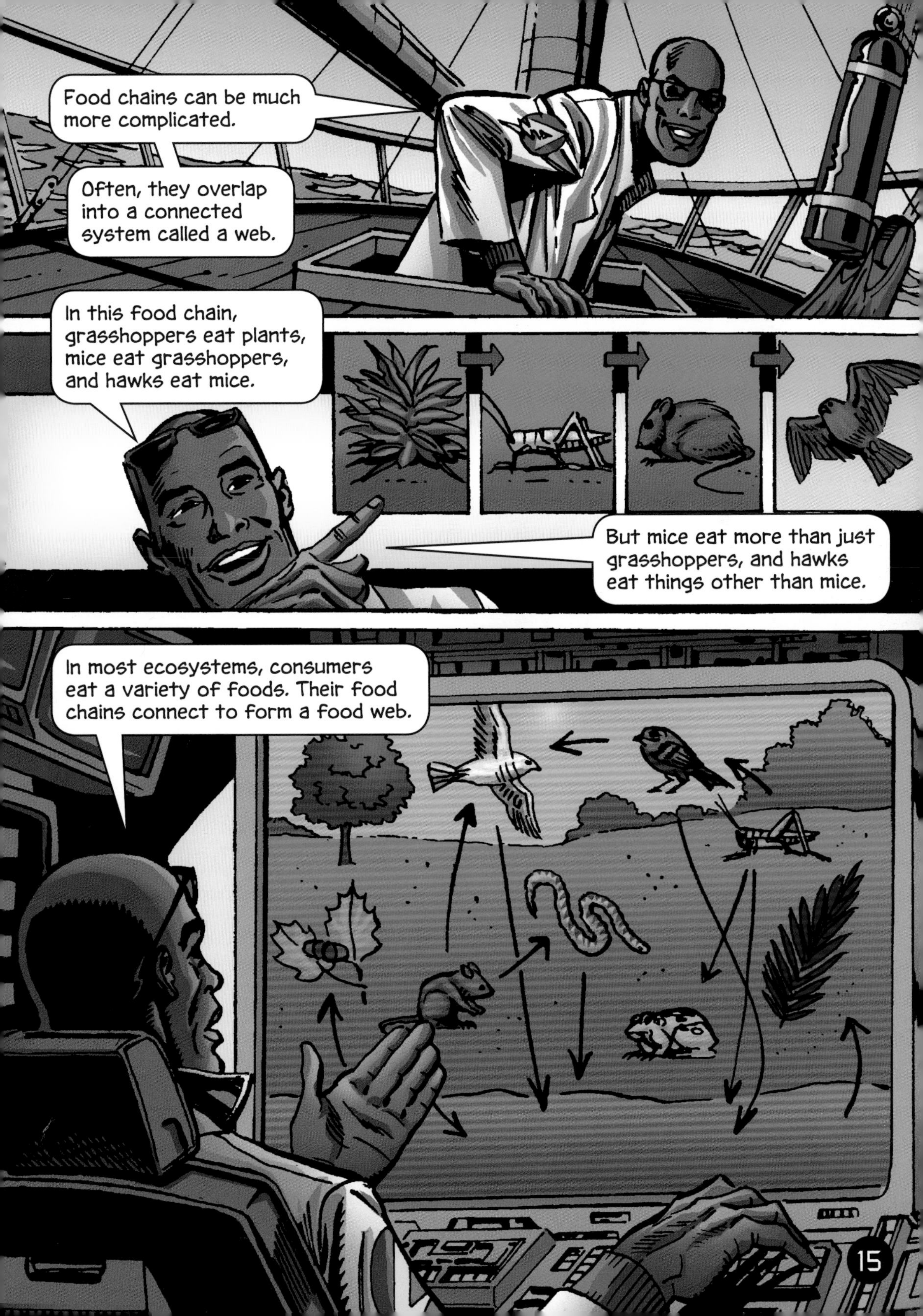

Food chains can be much more complicated.

Often, they overlap into a connected system called a web.

In this food chain, grasshoppers eat plants, mice eat grasshoppers, and hawks eat mice.

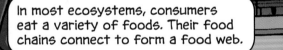

But mice eat more than just grasshoppers, and hawks eat things other than mice.

In most ecosystems, consumers eat a variety of foods. Their food chains connect to form a food web.

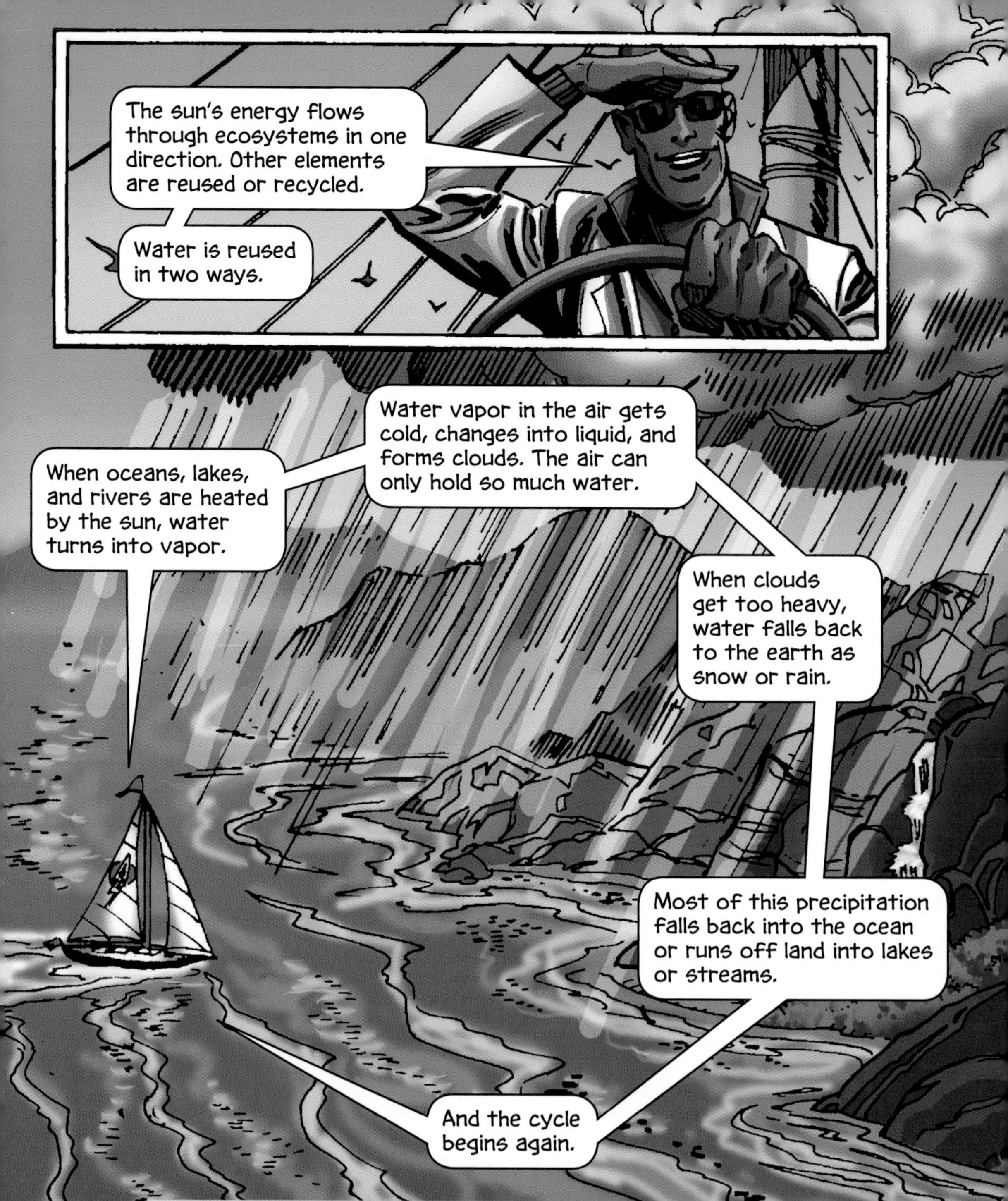
The sun's energy flows through ecosystems in one direction. Other elements are reused or recycled.
Water is reused in two ways.
When oceans, lakes, and rivers are heated by the sun, water turns into vapor.
Water vapor in the air gets cold, changes into liquid, and forms clouds. The air can only hold so much water.
When clouds get too heavy, water falls back to the earth as snow or rain.
Most of this precipitation falls back into the ocean or runs off land into lakes or streams.
And the cycle begins again.

DEFINITION

precipitation (pri-sip-i-TAY-shuhn)—water that falls from clouds to the earth's surface; precipitation can be rain, hail, sleet, or snow.

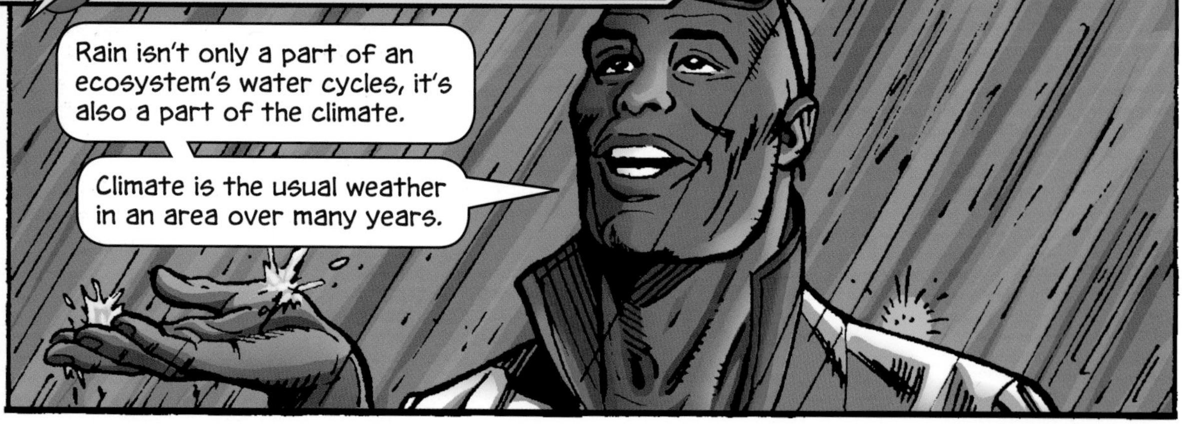
Rain isn't only a part of an ecosystem's water cycles, it's also a part of the climate.
Climate is the usual weather in an area over many years.

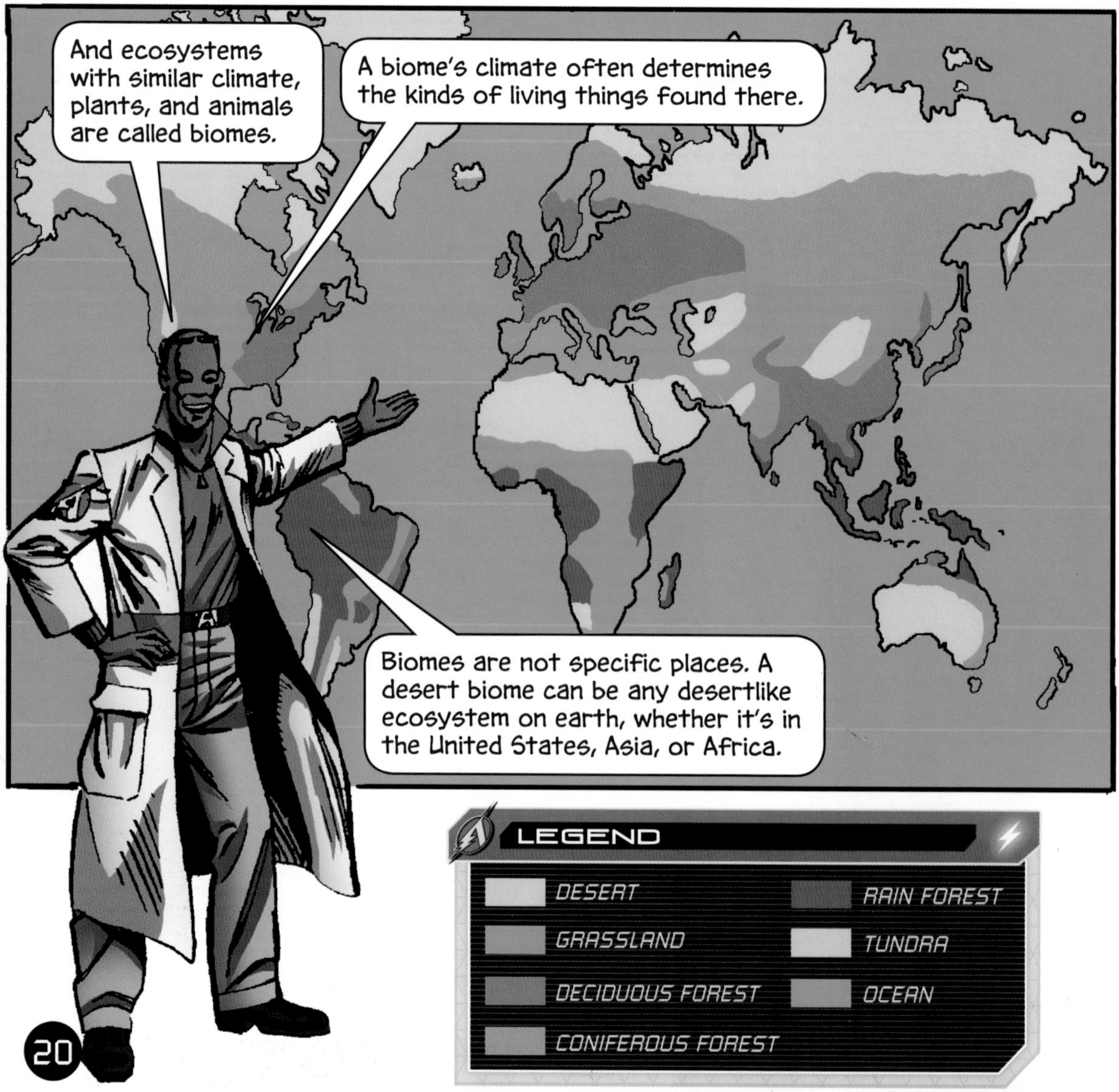
And ecosystems with similar climate, plants, and animals are called biomes.
A biome's climate often determines the kinds of living things found there.
Biomes are not specific places. A desert biome can be any desertlike ecosystem on earth, whether it's in the United States, Asia, or Africa.
LEGEND
DESERT
GRASSLAND
DECIDUOUS FOREST
CONIFEROUS FOREST
RAIN FOREST
TUNDRA
OCEAN

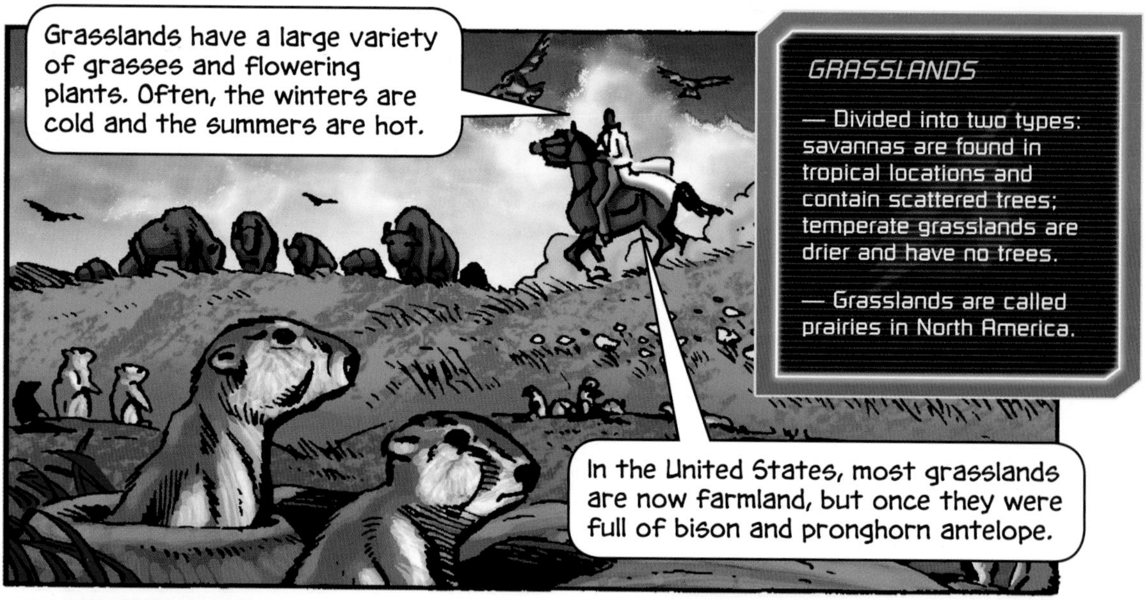
Grasslands have a large variety of grasses and flowering plants. Often, the winters are cold and the summers are hot.
GRASSLANDS
— Divided into two types: savannas are found in tropical locations and contain scattered trees; temperate grasslands are drier and have no trees.
— Grasslands are called prairies in North America.
In the United States, most grasslands are now farmland, but once they were full of bison and pronghorn antelope.

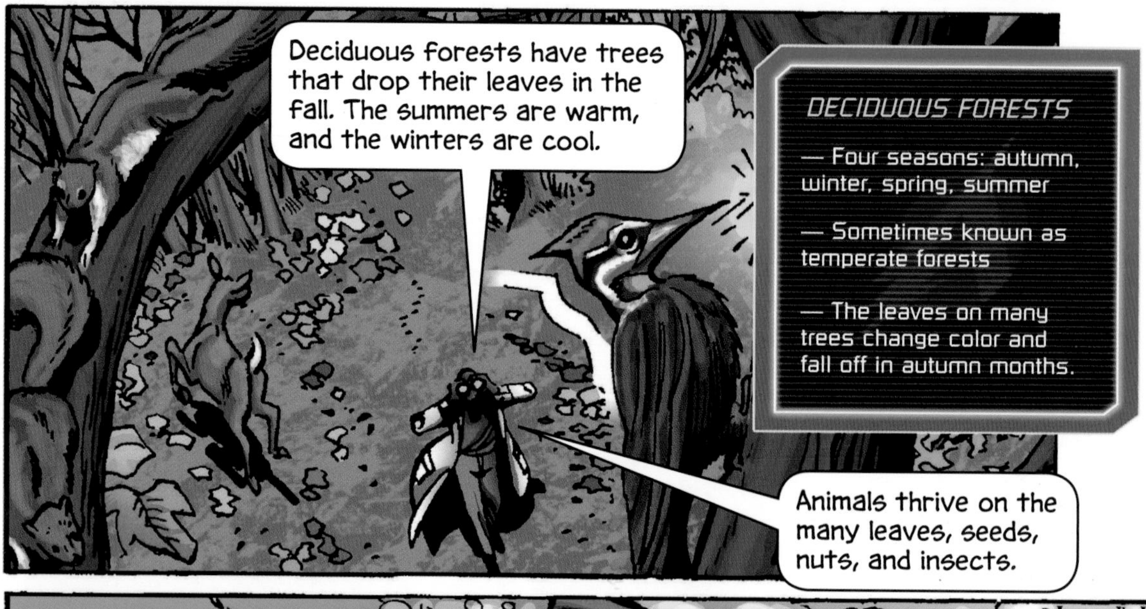
Deciduous forests have trees that drop their leaves in the fall. The summers are warm, and the winters are cool.
DECIDUOUS FORESTS
— Four seasons: autumn, winter, spring, summer
— Sometimes known as temperate forests
— The leaves on many trees change color and fall off in autumn months.
Animals thrive on the many leaves, seeds, nuts, and insects.

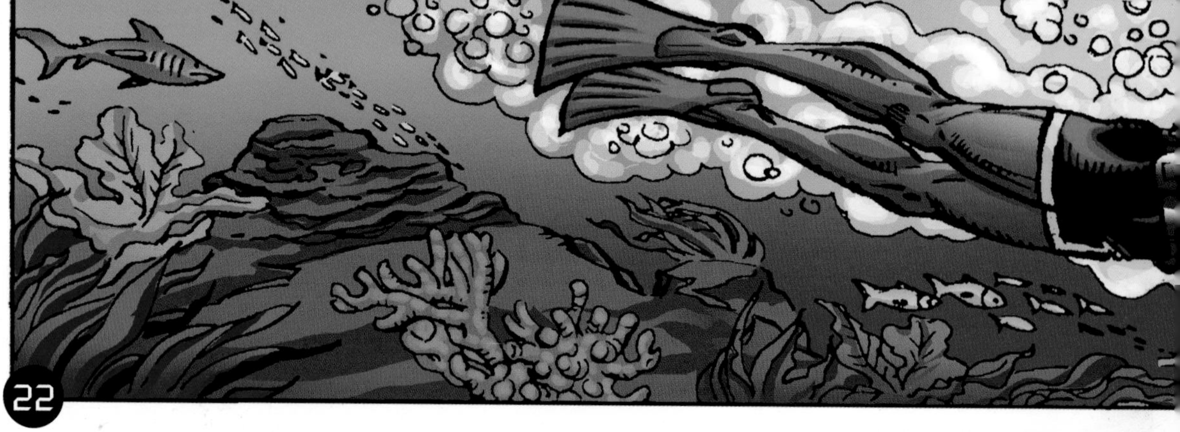

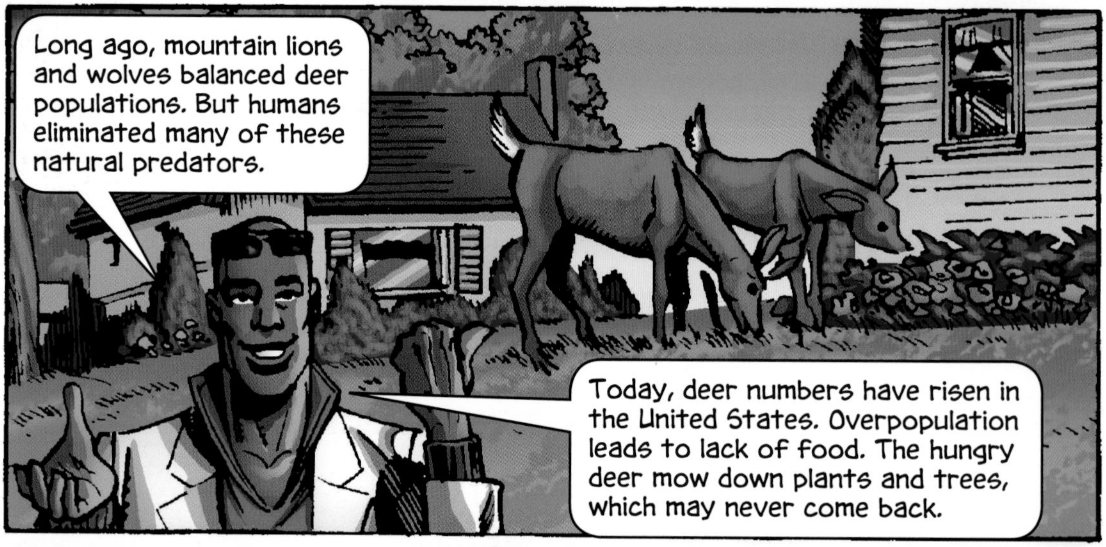
Long ago, mountain lions and wolves balanced deer populations. But humans eliminated many of these natural predators.
Today, deer numbers have risen in the United States. Overpopulation leads to lack of food. The hungry deer mow down plants and trees, which may never come back.

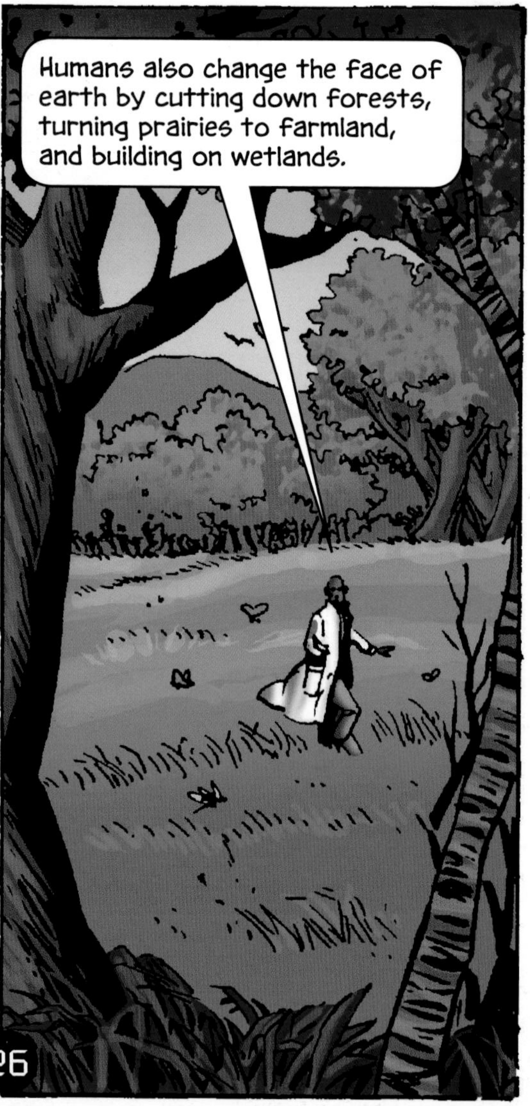
Humans also change the face of earth by cutting down forests, turning prairies to farmland, and building on wetlands.

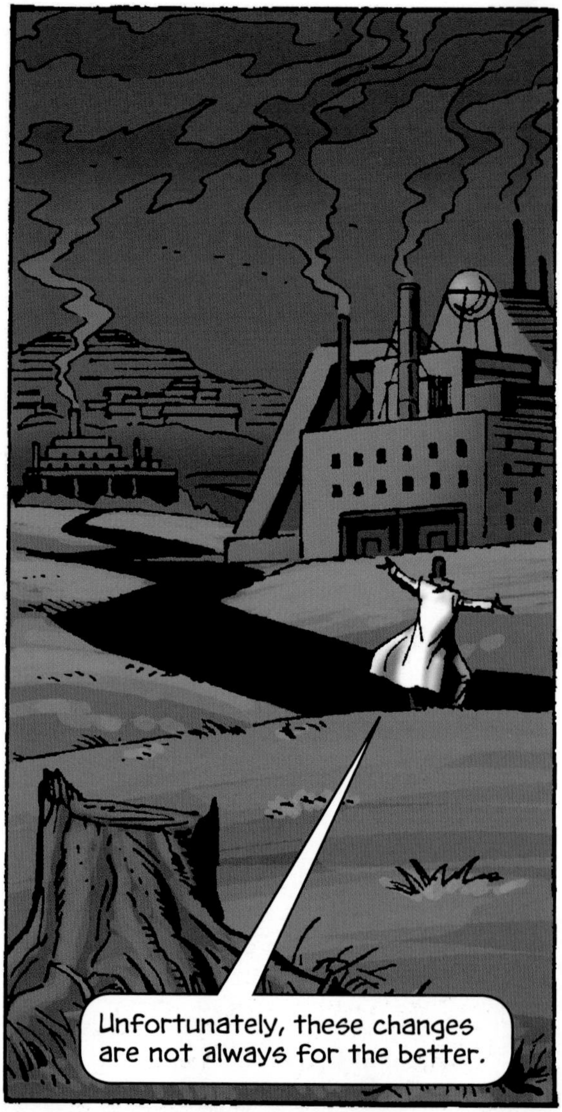
Unfortunately, these changes are not always for the better.

REDUCE YOUR IMPACT

You can protect the earth's ecosystems by practicing conservation. Use fewer natural resources like water and gas. Reduce waste and pollution whenever possible. Recycle bottles, cans, paper, and other recyclable materials.

MORE ABOUT ECOSYSTEMS

Ecosystems can be as large as an ocean or as small as a fishbowl. To identify the many ecosystems, some are named after their main feature, such as a pond ecosystem, a salt marsh ecosystem, or a redwood forest ecosystem.

Ecosystems are fragile, and alien invasive species can be a major problem. These plants and animals have been introduced to a part of the world where they don't belong. The brown tree snake was originally from Australia and Indonesia. Somehow, this sneaky reptile slithered onto a plane and hitched a ride to the island of Guam. With few predators on Guam, the tree snake has nearly wiped out native forest birds.

Believe it or not, the extinct passenger pigeon was once among the most numerous animals on earth. In the early 1800s, the passenger pigeon population was estimated at 1 to 5 billion birds. Huge, migrating flocks actually darkened the sky when they passed. Largely due to overhunting, the pigeons began to decline. By the 1890s, only small flocks were left. The last passenger pigeon, named Martha, died in the Cincinnati Zoo in 1914.

In the early 1990s, scientists tried to reproduce the ecosystems of earth inside a 3.5-acre (1.4-hectare) building called Biosphere 2. Located near Tucson, Arizona, the building contained a desert, a rain forest, and even a 900,000-gallon (3,406,860-liter) ocean. Some scientists believed buildings like Biosphere 2 could support life on the Moon or Mars. But after only two disappointing missions inside, the experiments ended. Today, visitors can tour the building and learn more about earth's fragile ecosystems.

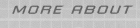 The rain forest is one of the largest biomes on earth. Sadly, more than 1.5 acres (.6 hectare) of rain forest are destroyed every second.

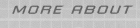 People should do their part every day to protect the environment. Several holidays throughout the year help keep us from forgetting this important task:

Earth Day (April 22)—celebrates clean air, land, and water

World Environment Day (June 5)—encourages environmental awareness worldwide

Arbor Day (different in each state)—promotes tree planting

MORE ABOUT

SUPER SCIENTIST

Real name: **Maxwell J. Axiom**
Hometown: **Seattle, Washington**
Height: **6' 1"**   Weight: **192 lbs**
Eyes: **Brown**   Hair: **None**

Super capabilities: Super intelligence; able to shrink to the size of an atom; sunglasses give x-ray vision; lab coat allows for travel through time and space.

Origin: Since birth, Max Axiom seemed destined for greatness. His mother, a marine biologist, taught her son about the mysteries of the sea. His father, a nuclear physicist and volunteer park ranger, schooled Max on the wonders of earth and sky.

One day on a wilderness hike, a megacharged lightning bolt struck Max with blinding fury. When he awoke, Max discovered a newfound energy and set out to learn as much about science as possible. He traveled the globe earning degrees in every aspect of the field. Upon his return, he was ready to share his knowledge and new identity with the world. He had become Max Axiom, Super Scientist.

GLOSSARY

carbon dioxide (KAHR-buhn dye-AHK-side)—a colorless, odorless gas that people and animals breathe out

community (kuh-MYOO-nuh-tee)—populations of people, plants, or animals that live together in the same area and depend on each other

ecology (ee-KOL-uh-jee)—the study of the relationships between plants and animals in their environments

environment (en-VYE-ruhn-muhnt)—the natural world of the land, water, and air

mate (MATE)—to join together for breeding

offspring (OFF-spring)—animals born to a set of parents

organism (OR-guh-niz-uhm)—a living plant or animal

population (pop-yuh-LAY-shuhn)—a group of people, animals, or plants living in a certain place

recycle (ree-SYE-kuhl)—the process of turning something old into something new

transpiration (transs-puh-RAY-shuhn)—the process by which plants give off moisture into the atmosphere

READ MORE

Harman, Rebecca. *Carbon-Oxygen and Nitrogen Cycles.*
Earth's Processes. Chicago: Heinemann, 2005.

Juettner, Bonnie. *Photosynthesis.* The KidHaven Science
Library. Detroit: KidHaven Press, 2005.

Kalman, Bobbie. *Food Chains and You.* Food Chains Series.
New York: Crabtree, 2005.

Petersen, Christine. *Conservation.* A True Book. New York:
Children's Press, 2004.

Spilsbury, Louise, and Richard Spilsbury. *The War in Your
Backyard: Life in an Ecosystem.* Chicago: Raintree, 2006.

INTERNET SITES

FactHound offers a safe, fun way to find Internet sites
related to this book. All of the sites on FactHound have been
researched by our staff.

Here's how:
1. Visit *www.facthound.com*
2. Choose your grade level.
3. Type in this book ID **0736868429** for
   age-appropriate sites. You may also browse
   subjects by clicking on letters, or by clicking on
   pictures and words.
4. Click on the **Fetch It** button.

FactHound will fetch the best sites for you!

INDEX